Simple Holiness

A Six-Week Walk on the Mountain of God

by

Albert E. Hughes, M.S., M.P.M.
Pastoral Counselor and Spiritual Director

and

Ronda Chervin
Professor of Philosophy and Spirituality

ENROUTE
Make the time

En Route Books and Media, LLC
5705 Rhodes Avenue
St. Louis, MO 63109

Cover credit: TJ Burdick

Library of Congress Control Number: 2018948425

Copyright © 2018 Albert E. Hughes and Ronda Chervin

All rights reserved.

ISBN-10: 1-7324148-2-3
ISBN-13: 978-1-7324148-2-2

Queries to: Ronda Chervin
(chervinronda@gmail.com)
or Albert E. Hughes (361)-834-4585

**Dedication
of
Albert E. Hughes**
for
Shannon, Katie, and Martha,
in memory of Gloria Jean Hughes,
daughter of the Most High

Ad Majorem Dei Gloriam

**Dedication
of
Ronda Chervin**
for
my family

CONTENTS

Introduction 1
   Why this Book? 7
   A Note to Leaders of Group Sessions 9
   How to Read this Book 10

Week I. Equip for a Mountain Walk .. 17

Week II. Determine if your Treasure Really Lies on the Mountain. 35

Week III. Find the Narrow Gate to the Mountain 45

Week IV. Obey the Commandments of God 61

Week V. Follow the Leading of God .. 77

Week VI. Love of God and Neighbor Unconditionally 97

VII. Remain on the Heights 115

Addenda 129

INTRODUCTION

Why This Book? – Albert E. Hughes

In a word, *frustration*. In two words, *resolved frustration*. I came to recognize God as person, rather than idea, at the age of 38. While we consider, accept, or reject ideas, *this* "idea" spoke to me directly, audibly. Five times. Yes, He did; and He confirmed His words in obvious ways, ultimately guiding me to becoming who I am today – an evangelist, retreat master, spiritual director, and author.

At God's clear direction, I began my journey into Catholicism, immediately to confront the word "holy" and the dictum, "All are called to holiness." So, I asked; I searched in a variety of ways, "What is it to be holy? How do I get to be holy?" The answers I got from priests or laity seemed to be vague, piecemeal and most often, seemed a put off: "Go and read the saints; go read saint whomever." I did that as free time and understanding allowed. Oh yes, I did that – to utter frustration.

In effect, I was finding trees – details: individual acts and effects of holiness; opinions of canonized saints and their biographers. Often, their experiences and tales and advice were expressed and influenced by the language and writing styles of their own era, which were to me foreign modes of a distant time and way of cultural understanding. Not that the holy masters of earlier times were found wanting, but . . . in the beginning, I didn't have the time or the formal education necessary to figure it all out.

<u>The Problem</u>. Those who commit to religious life or advanced religious study as a profession have the impetus and opportunity to concentrate their efforts toward overcoming these obstacles. But what about the rest of us? What about the doctors, lawyers, and Indian chiefs; plumbers and carpenters and housewives?

– in short, all the rest of us who are called to other demanding work. We all are called to holiness, but what is holiness in itself? And what must we do to approach it? And who has the time to answer these simple questions about simple holiness?

I could see the trees, but not the forest. Because of my military profession of systems engineering, management, and command, I was used to, expecting and looking in vain for a systematic, cohesive, *uncluttered* statement of holiness' essential features and a roadmap for attaining the same. Almost in the military format of a "point paper," the result of "completed staff work." I wanted the same *uncluttered* clarity of issues demanded by my military profession. I found useful clarity expressed in current terms and crisp logic – nowhere. It is no wonder that most Catholics assume holiness is reserved for the few and the mighty.

Early in my search, the only solid conclusion I reached was that holiness had to include relationship, not just technique. Holiness could only be achieved through relationship. It would take two to tango.

God and me.

My studies for the Master of Pastoral Ministry simply provided more information; more "trees" expressed in the definitions and theories of theology, psychology, counseling, and ethics. "Holiness" was not taught as a separate subject.

Still later, in a multi-year study leading to competence in spiritual direction, more of the same. More "trees". There always seemed to be an unspoken assumption that we students had a clear understanding of holiness' essence.

Finally, the uncluttered, simple essence of holiness became evident during my spiritual direction of Ronda Chervin. Out of the fog of detail, suddenly there emerged the whole clear, simple, glorious forest.

The Essence of and Way Toward Holiness

Sanctifying Grace is its indispensable basis, for grace unites man to God by allowing him to share in the divine life and is always accompanied by infused virtues and the gifts of the Holy Spirit (from *A*

Catholic Dictionary, Rockford, Illinois: Tan, 1997, p. 217).

Holiness may be approached – if we do our part, with six simple decisions well-acted upon with perseverance:

1) embrace Catholic faith and culture,
2) determine where your treasure lies,
3) find and enter the narrow gate,
4) obey the revealed will of God,
5) identify God's specific will for you, and
6) embrace unconditional charity.

You can do that!!! Of course, you can. Do you want to?

These six decisions, faithfully acted upon, include all the traditional approaches to holiness: humility, obedience, charity, and perseverance characteristic of the true disciple of Jesus Christ, in the love of the Father and the Holy Spirit. There is nothing taught here other than Christ's own teachings. The only difference is that he taught by parables and situational exhortations. We have taken a modern systematic approach. I will explain in sufficient, plain detail while my co-author, Ronda, will guide and encourage you in your understanding.

But be aware! There is a famous heresy called Pelagianism, based on the concepts of an English spiritual leader, Pelagius (360-418 A.D.). It seems he denied original sin and put the emphasis on free will as the main way to become holy. By contrast, the Church has always taught that we need divine grace to do the good in thought and deed. *Without me, you can do nothing.* (John 15:5) That does not mean that we don't have to cooperate with our free will when God offers us the grace to be good. Never think that we don't need to pray for the grace to do good since we easily can mess up on the simplest acts, given our fallen nature.

We don't create ourselves – God does. We can't save ourselves. God can.

Since God calls everyone to be holy, the emphasis in *Simple Holiness* is on our part in responding to God's grace. So, as you read, when you think about some step we present as just too difficult, don't give up. Just pray more for grace to become holy, specifically in the area of difficulty.

Why this book? That you might succeed in your own holy quest. You? Sure!

Why This Book? – Ronda Chervin

There are so many books about holiness. Many of the classics that Al found to be unhelpful, I found to be essential. Some such books about spirituality have been written by me. In one of my latest books, *The Way of Love* (St. Louis, Missouri: En Route Books and Media, 2017), I wrote that to be holy is to have nothing but love in our hearts: love of God, love of neighbor, love of beauty, love of truth; grateful love, sorrowful love, joyful love; with no bad anger, no excessive anxiety, no unforgiving bitterness, no despair, no complaining.

And yet, becoming the holy person I want to be eludes me.

I pray for it. I struggle against my habitual sins and flaws. I ask the holiest people I encounter for advice on how to be more holy. I know there are a few puzzle pieces missing, things that are required before I can be the kind of person I believe God wants me to be.

In 2017, at Corpus Christi, Texas, undergoing spiritual direction again, I was pessimistic, even if tremendously hopeful. Would Al Hughes, my latest spiritual director, find those missing puzzle pieces for me?

The biggest piece he found was the need to surrender to God my deepest fears. Now, I have and will continue to renounce the fear that wells up in my heart. In the course of our spiritual direction sessions, we wrote a book together, *Escaping Anxiety along the Road to Spiritual Joy* (St. Louis, Missouri: En Route Books and Media, 2018). And, as needed, Al still continues to advise.

Al's concepts promoting holiness, we believe, are inspired by the Holy Spirit. His concepts are far more encompassing than the elements of my problem with excessive anxiety. Wanting to share his truths with others seeking to grow in holiness, Al embarked on this book, *Simple Holiness*. My part is to provide reflection and commentary at the end of each chapter, along with suggestions for your personal reflection and possible group sharing.

Here is my prayer. *Father God, you would not call your children to holiness if it was an impossible goal. May the graces of the sacraments of Jesus, the inspiration of the Holy Spirit, and the intercession of Mother Mary and the saints remove obstacles in us to becoming the instruments of love you want so much for us to be.*

A Note to Leaders of Group Sessions

Simple Holiness is designed for individual readers. The authors believe that it also can be used with profit for small groups. So, if you are reading *Simple Holiness* with a view to leading such a group, we will provide questions for personal reflection and group sharing at the end of each chapter.

We think it would be beneficial to plan an introductory session including such features as these: sharing of names, phone numbers, and e-mails for leaders and participants; reading together the introduction and talking together about the questions for personal reflection and group sharing at the end of the introduction.

How to Read this Book – Albert Hughes

Young in my professional career, occasionally, I was advised, "Before you begin to climb the ladder of success, look up at the top rung and see if you really desire to go there." As you begin to consider this work, I suggest you do the same.

Do you really desire to climb the ladder of holiness? Do you seek a life of spiritual joy in union with God, no matter the ups and downs, the pains and disappointments of life? Do you want – in yourself - to approach the image and likeness of Christ? Do you want to "see" God? Do you want to be a true disciple of Jesus all the time?

As a preliminary step, visit the six rungs of the ladder and take a look. Read through this book completely. No skipping ahead! There is logic and instruction in the sequence. Perhaps you can read it in a weekend. If you get serious about holiness, then return to the beginning and prepare to walk the mountain of God.

If you begin most seriously, read and ruminate and pray and read again and decide and act to re-evaluate and transform your life according to each chapter. Take at least a week's repeated, daily study, prayer and reflection at each chapter. Try to incorporate the teachings in your life, at least in a preliminary way, before moving on to the next chapter. DO NOT SKIP ANYTHING. Stroll slowly about the mountain of God! No skipping lest you fall on rocky patches or slippery slopes!

We are aware how unlikely it is that someone will go from being a casual, even committed Christian to making a great advance in holiness in six or seven weeks. But you can read, reflect, learn, and perhaps make an initial commitment to the six necessary decisions in that time, through an understanding of their necessity and benefit. It will take time and persistence to develop habits of holiness.

Understand that to commit and persevere in the six necessary decisions we propose will be a life-time calling. Be encouraged that it gets easier as you proceed, as you first taste the joyful rewards! *My yoke is easy and my burden is light.*

Now, if you still harbor a modicum of doubt about God's reality, set that aside. The word is slow to get out, but most recently, the astrophysicist/cosmologist Roger Penrose, Ph.D., proved, in 1989, the necessary existence of God in scientific terms, using only scientific evidence. The battle of reason against faith is over. Faith won. As in any battle, there is some mopping up to be accomplished, but reason is now allied with faith. (For more on this, see *New Proofs for the Existence of God* by Fr. Robert J. Spitzer, SJ (Grand Rapids, Michigan: Wm. B. Eerdmans Publishing Co., 2010)). Here is an interesting quotation from an American astrophysicist, Bruce L. Garden:

> *"(When)...the proof that there was an absolute beginning to any universe... (is) conjoined with the fact that our universe...exists and its conditions are fine-tuned immeasurably beyond the capacity of any mindless process, the*

scientific evidence points inexorably toward transcendent intelligent agency as the most plausible, if not the only, reasonable explanation."

A final enjoinder. Holiness is a goal, not a condition of arrival. Never call yourself holy. Very few reach the top of the mountain this side of permanent residency in heaven. If another should refer to you as holy, it can only be a term relative to the speaker. Thank them gently for their kindness, but do not accept their judgment. There is always more progress to be made.

While the understanding of the essence of holiness and the decision process I propose is my own understanding of Holy Spirit guidance, I strongly urge you to pay diligent attention to Ronda's commentary, her reflections, and the questions she proposes for your consideration, either alone or (preferably) in group discussions.

Group discussions after individual readings would be most beneficial. In my 25 years of teaching Catholicism and Scripture, I often noticed that in class discussion, the truth of an issue was resident in the collective student body. While each individual had a different piece of the truth, through discussion with patience, the whole truth would emerge. I am confident you will find that as well. I urge you. After individual reading, discuss in a small group of readers.

For Personal Reflection and Group Sharing

- What is your definition of holiness?
- Has there been an evolution of your view of holiness over time?
- Describe people you think of as holy who you have known personally or through reading, TV, and films.
- Did any introductory insights of Al Hughes and/or Ronda Chervin challenge you?
- What do you hope to learn from reading *Simple Holiness?*

"...spiritual growth comes from reading and reflection. By reading we learn what we did not know; by reflection we retain what we have learned. Reading...

confers two benefits. It trains the mind to understand...it turns man's attention from the follies of the world and leads him to love of God."

- St. Isidore, Bishop (560-636) from the *Book of Maxims*

WEEK I

Equip for a Mountain Walk

Listen to me, ye who live in the senses
And think through the senses only:

Immortality is not a gift,

Immortality is an achievement;

And only those who strive mightily
Shall achieve it.

- Edgar Lee Masters (1868-1950)

People go to church for varied reasons. They range from those forced to go out of parental, spousal, or social pressure – they don't want to be there – to those who participate fully in the life of the Church in many varied ways. Some, especially the younger, are where I was thirty years ago; confused by the "trees" of detail, not seeing the "forest". Matters of work, personal interest, or other circumstances prevent their further study. Some associate holiness only with canonized saints. Not comprehending the way, they balk: it's too difficult to be a saint.

And there are those who believe most Christians are merely posturing to make you think they are better than they are! But consider this. We go to school to learn arithmetic which is the foundation for algebra, which is the foundation for trigonometry, which is the foundation for analytical geometry and calculus, etc. We don't start with calculus or beyond and work down to 2+2=4.

In like manner, we embrace the Catholic church and culture as the foundation and exercise for finding where our treasure lies, which leads to finding the narrow gate mentioned by Jesus; which leads us truly to obey God's will, which urges us on to unconditional charity, which leads us – if we persevere – to a measure of sanctity.

Catholic church and culture is the beginning, the foundation, not the peak of sanctity.

In building a bell tower, we do not start with the cupola and bell; we start with the foundation. We don't start by walking down the mountain of God from on high; don't walk downslope toward the valley of the shadow of death.

Decision #1:
To Equip for the Walk on the Mountain of God.

I was glad when they said to me, "Let us go to the house of the Lord!" You that stand in the house of the Lord, in the courts of the house of our God; come, bless the Lord, all you servants of the Lord who stand by night in the house of the Lord! Lift up your hands to the holy place, and Bless the Lord.
- From the Psalms 122, 135 and 134

You may, already, be well equipped for your walk on the mountain of God. Consider: to what extent have you embraced

Catholic life and culture? Let's check the basic equipment list for your back pack. You may think you know all these basics and that you just can skip ahead. Instead, pause as you read thanking God for each of these gifts that you do have! And you might be surprised by certain oversights.

Sacraments

Sacraments are worth reviewing. They are the foundational conduit of grace for most Christians, essential to every quest for authentic Christian life. They provide initial relationship with God, essential preparation for a walk on the mountain. There are seven. Unless you seek priesthood, you will need four or five: Baptism, Confirmation, Confession, Eucharist; perhaps if you choose, Matrimony. About to die or are seriously ill? Inquire of your priest for Anointing of the Sick.

What is a sacrament? A visible sign of an invisible reality. Too many people see the obviously visible and forget there is something else going on. Grace. Grace is an unearned, free gift of God. Along with the visible water of <u>Baptism</u>, you get the Holy Spirit. This is your adoption as a child of God. <u>Confirmation</u> is your intellectual acknowledgement and acceptance of the gift and your commitment to live a Christian life as an adopted child of God. Grace follows. The holy oils of Confirmation are accompanied by additional grace to strengthen you in your life in Christ. Still, you must cooperate with grace. <u>Confession,</u> you know, is your chance before God to identify your sins and start over with a clean slate when you fall short. More grace received there assists you to conquer habitual sin.

<u>Eucharist</u> is the consecrated flesh and blood of Christ, which we consume at Mass. You have heard it said, "You are what you eat." Crudely put, but true. Through frequent reception of the Eucharist, expect transformation!

Some may protest, "But that obviously is only a wafer of unleavened bread and a sip of wine." Christ says differently.

Very truly, I tell you, unless you eat the flesh of the Son of Man and drink His blood, you have no life in you. Those who eat my flesh and drink my blood have eternal life, and I will raise them up on the last day; for my flesh is true food and my blood is true drink. Those who eat my flesh and drink my blood abide in me, and I in them. Just as the living Father sent me, and I live because of the Father, so whoever eats me will live because of me.

- John 6: 53-57

Clear enough? The appearance is obvious. The actual substance (reality) normally is not so obvious. However, from time to time, the Lord reminds the wavering in his church. Not often, but visible to those present from time to time, hosts will bleed real blood or transform into actual human flesh. Books are published listing many such miracles. Here are two recent instances.

In 1998 at the Vatican, during a semi-private Mass with Saint John Paul II, Pope, a host being offered to the guest of honor suddenly sagged and revealed its true nature as a piece of fresh flesh. At least a dozen present witnessed the miracle. This author heard the testimony of a priest who, on an occasion in this country, witnessed a bleeding host early in this century. Many such events have occurred over the years. The most spectacular reminder occurred in the 8th century.

During a Mass, before the startled eyes of a doubting monk priest, the Sacred Host visibly changed into a circle of Flesh. The consecrated wine was transformed into bright red blood that coagulated into five small clots. Christ's Flesh and Blood from that instance still exist in a fresh state after nearly 1300 years. Modern medical investigations conclude the flesh is heart muscle, with the same AB type as the blood. Neither has been kept in a sealed container of inert gas and neither has any traces of a preservative agent. For nearly 1300 years!

Intrigued? Look up the Eucharistic Miracle of Lanciano, Italy. The same blood type, I read, is on the Shroud of Turin and the Veil of Veronica.

The point of this Eucharistic refresher? Despite our religious and ministerial training, our many years working with converts, the young, the elderly, the sick, and the dying; for a long time my wife and I were routinely only Sunday mass goers – other than for special occasions. Finally, we decided to attend daily Mass as much as possible, i.e., receive nearly daily Eucharist.

It was like punching the accelerator of my turbo-Buick. A bit of a lag, then WOW! Transformative power. I can't describe it further, but you also may experience it if you go to Mass daily or as often as you can. There with frequent mass, you will also find like-minded people who are attempting to go beyond some minimum. They will teach and support you with their lives to the best of their ability.

Sacramentals

If a guest enters your home, can they tell you are Catholic? Example: Someone entering our house immediately saw on the wall to their left four icons of various saints. Straight ahead, more of the same, with saint Mary prominent. They don't see it immediately, but they were under a cross as they stood on the threshold. To their right a framed document, an ornate blessing of our 25th anniversary signed by Saint John Paul II, Pope. All the rooms contained similar artifacts.

My wife died two years ago, but my little apartment, today, has the same cross over the door and some of the same articles as before, including an immediately seen olive wood crucifix.

The point? Sacramental artifacts announce a witness to others and remind all present of the constant presence of God. Upon entering our house, people sensitive to the Spirit, whether laborers or professionals, would sometimes stand in the living room in awe or quietly mention their sense that Mary was present, or simply mention a feeling of profound peace. *Where two or more are gathered, ...*

Ronda, since her conversion in 1959, always wears a rather large crucifix around her neck visible outside her clothing. This used to be the practice of every Catholic. It provides instant evangelization without words.

Faith, Prayer, and Petition

If you have come this far, I need not say much about faith and prayer, except to remind you of the importance of a daily prayer life.

"I do not mean the prayer of outward observance but prayer from the heart, not confined to fixed times or periods but continuous throughout the day and night. Our spirits should be quick to reach out toward God...when carrying out its duties, caring for the needy, performing works of charity, giving generously in the service of others. Prayer stands before God as an honored ambassador. It gives joy to the spirit, peace to the heart. I speak of prayer, not words. In this way you will make your spirit a perfect dwelling place for the Lord...and through his grace you will already possess him...in the temple of your spirit."

- St. John Chrysostom, Bishop

I attend and recommend Mass (the greatest prayer) five times a week. Seven if you can. Some do not have daily access to a Mass. Do as much as you can.

At my church, the daily Mass is at noon. In the morning, a wakeup cup of coffee (dark roast, chicory, and cream, please) followed by the liturgy of the hours. I use the four-volume set complete with hymns, scripture, and wonderful writings of the Church fathers and saints. Then, spontaneous chats with God throughout the day as I go about my business. Informal witness at every opportunity.

But a special note about "petition". If you want something, particularly in the vein of increased faith and holiness – ask for it in prayer. Whatever it is, you will have it if God so wills. In his time. (As an agnostic, when I asked for faith, the gift took nearly five years to arrive! But then it came with dramatic impact.)

There is your checklist by way of example. Wordy, I admit, but just sufficient. If your backpack is similarly equipped, though not identical, if you are fully engaged in Catholic life and culture, as described, you are ready to walk on the mountain of God.

Catholic Life and Culture; Weigh Stop or Destination?

You are ready, but do you desire? Is there fire in your gut? Do you desire holiness more than merely a comfortable or routine or familiar life? So far, we have described "good" Catholic practice. But you can be more. If you continue, the challenge will be to persevere. The path can be steep; you will fall occasionally on the loose and slippery rocks of sin or inattention, but press on. The rewards are great.

Listen to Fr. Georges Florovsky, quoted in *The Orthodox Way,* by Bishop Kallistos Ware (Crestwood, New York: S. Vladimir's Seminary Press, 1995, p. 1)

The Church gives us not a system, but a key; not a plan of God's City, but the means of entering it. Perhaps someone will lose his way because he has no plan. But all that he will see, he will see without a mediator, he will see it directly, it will be real for him; while he who has studied only the plan risks remaining outside and not really finding anything.

You *could* stop now. Catholic life and culture is a pleasant destination, but make it only a way stop and move on to the pursuit of holiness. You will be amazed! Climb the mountain! Ronda?

Ronda's Encouragement

In my autobiography, *En Route to Eternity,* (New York: The Miriam Press, 1994), I describe my conversion in 1959 from being an atheist philosophy student to becoming an ardent Catholic at age twenty-one.

I was brought into the Church by the circle of Catholics surrounding the famous philosopher, Dietrich Von Hildebrand. All the Catholics in his circle wanted to be holy.

When I became a Catholic, I was surprised that there were many others who didn't have such a goal. They might have many virtues, some I didn't have myself. But, they seemed to think of religion as a segment of their lives along with other aspects such as their jobs, their hobbies, their recreational pursuits.

My group thought of God as the absolute center of our lives with whom we were to try to be close every moment day and night by means of daily Mass, monthly confession, prayer, the rosary, spiritual reading, and trying to love others unselfishly.

Especially, daily Mass was the practice. Later, I found in the *Catechism of the Catholic Church* (CCC 133), "Christ Jesus...is present in many ways to his Church..., but most especially in the Eucharist." We should go to daily Mass unless it is overly difficult due to the only church being far away, family needs, travel, illness, extreme weather, etc. In the latter part of my life, more and more Eucharistic adoration is important to me, as well.

(Now a dedicated widow, daily Mass is part of my rule of life. I like to explain it with this literary image, If Jesus wants to leap down from Heaven through the words of the priest into my body, shouldn't I be there to receive Him?)

With the group around Von Hildebrand, I was acutely was aware of my own failure to be holy most of the time. This was manifested primarily by fits of anger when frustrated and also by so much distraction at Mass and in prayer that I didn't feel especially close to God.

Ten years after my baptism, closeness to

God in prayer grew by leaps and bounds after coming into the graces of the charismatic gifts of the Holy Spirit. When I became a Catholic professor, writer and speaker, more insights came as I tried to figure out the nature of virtue and vice so as to communicate such truths to others.

Truth about holiness came to me through reading the lives of the saints, the writings of the spiritual masters, and writing many books about saints, myself. (See www.rondachervin.com for more information about these books of mine.)

In terms of the theme of this book, *Simple Holiness,* you might find it intriguing that Dietrich Von Hildebrand, the philosophical leader of the group that brought me into the Church, used to proclaim: "There is an abyss between an ardent Catholic and a saint."

What is the difference? I think of it as having to do with the total surrender a saint makes to Jesus so that his or her thoughts, words, and deeds emanate God's love. Striking contemporary images can be found when reading about St. Padre Pio or St. Teresa of Calcutta.

By contrast, an ardent Catholic such as myself still has pockets of pride, expressed in anger when things don't go my way, and pockets of anxiety coming from lack of trust in God.

This is why, even at age eighty, not yet a saint, I want to drink in the wisdom of my current spiritual director, Al Hughes, whom I think is higher than I up the mountain of God.

A note about spiritual direction: it is very beneficial to have a spiritual director. That is a priest, sister, brother, or lay person who undertakes to guide you prayerfully in your growth in holiness, without cost, usually once a month, but more often if convenient. And especially in times of crisis. But since these can be hard to find, the next best thing is to talk often with a good friend whom you regard as holier than yourself.

For Personal Reflection and Group Sharing

- Trace your experience of the sacraments through the years.

- Did any insights of Al Hughes in this chapter give you tools for your walk on the mountain of God?
- Do you think of yourself as a good Catholic? An ardent Catholic? A wannabe saint?
- Compose a prayer for yourself for your walk upon the mountain of God.

"I perceive that I am dealt with by superior powers. This is a pleasure, a joy, an existence which I have not procured myself. I speak as a witness on the stand and tell what I have perceived."
- Henry David Thoreau

WEEK II

Determine if your Treasure Really Lies on the Mountain

... what would be happiness to clear minds would be a torment to those that are defiled. Therefore, let the mists of worldly vanities be dispelled.... Love of the world cannot be reconciled with love of God, and the man who does not separate himself from the children of this generation cannot join the company of the sons of God.
- Saint Leo the Great, Pope.

Decision #2:
To Determine Where Your Treasure Lies.

Saint Leo refers to two types of people, those who are in the world and of it, and those who are in the world, but not of it. He could have started out by saying "There are two types of people in the world..." followed by his explanation. On occasion, we may hear something quite similar in casual conversation today.

I remember this rendition, which I first heard in high school. "There are three types of people; those who seek power, those who seek truth, and those who just go along so as to get along." Matthew and Luke writing today might well have started by writing, "There are four types of people; ..."

This is precisely the issue Jesus faced as told us in the story of his temptation in the desert. (Matthew 4 and Luke 4.) The story is written for all the ages and therefore is slightly vague of meaning to any particular time. The devil suggests that Jesus "Turn this stone into bread...," or "Worship me and all the nations will be yours...," and even "Jump off the temple tower, for God will protect you from harm!" That represents three types of people; the fourth type are those who don't listen to the devil, tell him to buzz off, as Jesus politely did by quoting scripture.

So, to what, exactly, do these temptations refer? The temptation to convert stone into bread represents wealth. If today, a kid comes up to you in the street and says, "Gimme some bread, man!" you know immediately that he wants your money!

The second is obvious. The offer to control the nations represents power over others.

The third is less obvious, but represents the easy life. "No harm will come to you." This includes a life free from challenges, free from suffering, free from all manner of hardship, free from toil, free from criticism or persecution, which may include an easy life without accomplishments (sloth). This is a person who plays it safe all the way through, accomplishing little, going along with anything, just to get along.

There you have it. There are four types of people. Those who seek wealth, those who seek power, and those who seek the easy life. The fourth are those who seek holiness. Your most precious treasure variously may be wealth, power, the easy life, or pursuit of God, i.e. holiness!

So, which is your most precious treasure? If you have truly searched your heart and find one of the first three has your heart, but you desire holiness, then it is time to explore the virtue of detachment.

Detachment

An ascetic indifference to creatures, not absolute but relative to the affection had for God and divine things. True detachment consists not in a negation of affection for creatures (all of which have their part in God) but rather in an enlightened and just sense of proportion. It is exercised in respect to material success, wealth, "good fortune", not because these things are not good in their kind or degree but on account of their difference in kind and relative importance in the destiny of the human being considered as a whole.
- *A Catholic Dictionary*, p. 144

Note: In this definition, "creature" refers to all creation, not only animals. "Ascetic" refers to a disciplined life.

smoke!

My experience is that we can think that we are not eager for wealth or power or an easy life, but our temptations and defects of character can be more subtle than engaging in mortal sins of theft, ruthless ambition, or laziness.

Several examples come to mind: parents who could live on one income if they had only what was necessary but who are overly attached to such luxuries as a TV in each room, three cars, etc., etc., etc. Both parents work to provide these and other luxuries, but have fewer children than if one of the parents remained at home during the day.

Or, someone works at a job that involves grey areas of fraud such as being a realtor who conceals important missing or defective features in houses when selling them to homebuyers. (Not to suggest that all realtors are like that.)

Easy-life choices could be something so seemingly minor as usually finishing up whatever one is doing even if it makes us late for obligatory appointments. The victim is the person waiting for sometimes half an hour for us to arrive at the planned time. The feeling is, my time counts, and the other person's time does not matter.

Another way of asking ourselves where our treasure lies that I find helpful is this: is my love for God the center of my life, or more just the most important segment? If only the most important segment, vs. the center, then I easily can juggle priorities so that some choices that are not really God's will take precedence. Men may recognize this tendency as a carry-over from their work of compartmentalization of thoughts and actions – a common and necessary part of work life.

Now, of course, God's will in daily life is not always clear and we don't want to become scrupulous. Scrupulosity is making things that are not obligatory into strict rules. Examples: thinking that we have to go to a weekend Mass even if we are feverish. Or being miserly about possessions that really are God's will, such as buying a keyboard for a child with musical talent. Other choices are much clearer. Should I visit my brother who was just taken to the hospital after an accident, or watch my favorite TV serial, instead?

Here are some examples from my own life that reveal that my treasure is not always showing love for God over other goods when there is a conflict. I will often recount juicy stories about others when it would be more holy to inquire compassionately about the problem my friends might want to talk about. Pursuing work tasks without praying for the grace to do them in a loving spirit, resulting in fits of anger when things don't go my way. Enjoying harsh judgment of those with whom I disagree in order to feel superior and victorious even if just only in my own head.

For Personal Reflection and Group Sharing

- Are there any ways that you value wealth over the "poverty" of having only necessities?
- Do you complain about working at a job that has little power position because you wish too much to be the boss?

- Do you evaluate your day by how easy it went vs. how much love you showed to others?
- You might go through the day noticing whenever angry, depressed, or anxious feelings come up when there in issues about money, power, or ease?

St. Paul writes in Philippians 3: 1-16, "But those things I used to consider gain, I have now reappraised as loss in the light of Christ. I have come to rate all as loss in the light of the surpassing knowledge of my Lord, Jesus Christ. For his sake I have forfeited everything; I have accounted all else rubbish, so that Christ may be my wealth and I may be in him..."

WEEK III

Find the Narrow Gate to the Mountain

Go within his gates, giving thanks. Enter his courts with songs of praise. Give thanks to him and bless his name. Who shall climb the mountain of the Lord? Who shall stand in his holy place? The man with clean hands and pure heart, who...has not sworn so as to deceive his neighbor.
— Psalm 24

Enter through the Narrow Gate; for the gate is wide and the road easy that leads to destruction; and there are many who take it. For the gate is narrow and the road is hard that leads to life, and there are few who find it.
— Mt 7: 13

Decision #3:
To Find and Enter the Narrow Gate.

I am delighted you are here, joining me at the base of God's mountain, at the edge of the valley of the shadow of death. Together, you and I will find the narrow gate. Jesus warns us against the wide gate; recommends the narrow gate. For many it is hard to find – many do not even look for it. Yet, it is close by. You and I will find the narrow gate, shortly.

In my first years of Faith, I ran across Matthew 7:13 (quoted above). I had no clue. What did this mean; what is and where was the narrow gate? I asked a few fellow Catholics on Andrews Air Force Base where my wife, my children, and I lived in my early days of faith, but they had no answer. I stopped asking, realizing that none of them ever seriously had considered Matthew 7: 13. But it haunted me. I did not want to "come to Jesus" and still not *enter through the narrow gate.*

The issue sank from constant concern, but cropped up occasionally, in passing. It remained unresolved during my year of formal Scripture studies at Seattle University, in my avocational work as a Scripture teacher and retreat master, and in my studies devoted to the art of spiritual direction. I knew the narrow gate was a metaphor, but that did not answer the question.

Finally, in my practice of spiritual direction, in assisting others, the light lit. The answer was there all along. It had been expressed indirectly over and over in studies, readings, and Masses since my conversion. But not as a complete "narrow gate" image. My wife, Jeannie, and I had passed through the narrow gate early in the 1980's without realizing it as such.

Jesus, I have read, was using an actual gate in the wall of old Jerusalem as an analogy. There was in the first century a very low and narrow opening built into the wall; so narrow and low that a camel would have to kneel, be unloaded of all baggage, and then crawl on his knees to get through.

In another passage Jesus refers to a camel passing through "the eye of the needle," an apparent reference to the common name of the same gate. In each case, by the narrow gate he was inferring that we had to unload our excess baggage of sin to follow him. The analogy still applies. This, following, is what I now realize.

Enter through the narrow gate.... At first, the narrow gate is completely obscured and bound by the weeds and choking vines of sin. The word "sin" has fallen on many a deaf ear these days, but call it what you will, the effects are real; sins are an offense against God *and* against yourself. If not recognized, repented, and corrected, they may lead through the wide gate; they can lead to self-destruction.

Especially, sins are like tall weeds and vines that hide and bind the narrow gate: false pride and covetousness and lust and anger and gluttony and envy and spiritual sloth; each with many personal variations. (Spiritual sloth is living with little conscious concern and attention to practice of religious truths, sacramental life, and the commands of God; i.e. leading a secular life, "of the world," as is often said.)

My long experience as catechist, retreat master, and spiritual director suggests that all of us have a problem with at least one of these listed sins, often resulting in an addiction to a greater or lesser degree. Most common in our time and culture seem to be sexual lust, excess body-weight (gluttony), and spiritual sloth.

Each of the listed sins can develop into choking domination of one's life. They cause us to turn in on ourselves in self-righteousness, self-pity, anger, resentment, and addiction to self-destructive habits. (Addictions in all forms come to mind.) If not resisted, they can lead toward death of soul if they become mortal. Grace received through repeated sacramental confession is your weapon of choice.

A sin is mortal, let us be reminded by St Thomas Aquinas, if the sin is in regard to a serious matter, is freely committed by the perpetrator, and is willfully committed with full knowledge. Mortal sins equate to complicit self-destruction.

Nevertheless, venial sins can have similar, if not mortal effects. Lesser sins might be such acts as idle gossip, taking something of little consequence not belonging to you, mild detraction from someone's reputation, angry unloving outbursts, overeating, drinking too much alcohol, and driving drunk, etc. The problem is, venial sins can lead to mortal sins if the misbehavior becomes normal to your behavior.

If you have little or no control over an addiction, and you are not committing the associated sin freely, you are likely not in mortal sin. Your confessor will have the final word. Again, grace received through repeated sacramental confession is your weapon of choice. Failure to seek confession and professional help for habitual sins is definitely an impediment to holiness.

The blessedness of seeing God is justly promised to the pure of heart. For the eye that is unclean would not be able to see the brightness of the true light, and what would be happiness to clear minds would be a torment to those who are defiled. Therefore, let the mists of worldly vanities be dispelled, and the inner eye be cleansed of all the filth of wickedness, so that the soul's gaze may feast serenely upon the great vision of

God. Saint Leo the Great, Pope.

Everyone comes equipped with or soon acquires the seeds of sin. The theologian blames original sin. *This* is a manifestation of original sin: that in infancy, we demand only our own physical wants and needs. Natural enough and essential for the infant; therewith, life begins and persists in self-absorption, lacking in degrees of love for God and neighbor. The altruistic commands of God have to be both taught and acted upon.

To find the narrow gate, first identify your own sin(s): whether they derive from false pride, covetousness, lust, anger, gluttony, envy, or spiritual sloth. Identify your personal weeds of sin that obscure; the vines that bind the narrow gate. To find and enter the narrow gate, you have to cut away the weeds and vines of sin with the assistance of grace through a steady program of sacramental confession. This is a lifetime task.

We are never totally without sin, scripture tells us, but frequent confession and serious efforts toward clearing away most sins should enable you to approach the narrow gate. It is unlocked; but even if unbound of sin, still hard to open. Its two hinges are corroded from neglect, for... *there are few who find it.*

This is what you will find. The gate is named charity. We will consider its name completely at Week VI. The upper hinge is named obedience. This hinge needs both Week IV and Week V to consider fully. So, we begin now to consider and free the lower hinge. The lower hinge is called humility. Naturally, it is freed with the oil of humility.

Humility often is presented as a character weakness, but weakness of character is not humility. It simply is weakness of character. The authentically humble person is not a pawn or a punching bag for the "strong," the assertive, the controlling, or the authoritative person. Often, the authentically humble person is the truly strong person in the room. Humility is not about weakness, it is about truth. It is...

...an appreciation and external expression of (a person's) true position

with respect to God and his neighbor; opposed, therefore, both to pride and to immoderate self-abjection. (It) is an absolutely necessary prerequisite and the first of the virtues to the extent that it removes the greater obstacles to faith, upon which all rests.

But affected humility is odious and the virtue does not require that a man should deprecate his ability...(but) consists in keeping oneself within one's own bounds, neither narrower nor wider than they really are.

- A Catholic Dictionary, p. 239

Not the church doormat – but that humility expressed by living forthrightly within one's realistic capacities and limitations; one's true place, gifts, and conditions. Neither to seek and grasp beyond reality, nor to waste real capacities on habitual distractions or sloth. This doesn't mean that no one should ever enjoy recreation but always within moderation.

A sad example of grasping beyond reality. As a very young Lieutenant, I talked my way into being elected Commodore of a start-up yacht club. It was a real ego-power trip. Until I realized I had neither acquired the skills to take command of club promotion and growth, nor the time away from my Air Force career to work the problem. I was all talk, or as we say in Texas, "All hat and no cattle." I resigned and left the club, humiliated. To paraphrase Pearl Bailey, "I've been humble and I've been humiliated, and honey, humble is better!" (Pearl was a jazz singer famous in the 1930's. She was quoted as saying, "I've been rich and I've been poor; and honey, rich is better!")

Nothing written here forbids the realistic increase of your capacities through study, work, and contemplation. As the Army slogan says, "Be all that you can be!" Attain self-knowledge and live within the assessment of who you really are. Authentic humility is the basis of all virtue.

A more positive personal example: My parents and teachers encouraged me to pursue a Ph.D. Especially, my mother wanted me to live out her unrealized dream; to become a professor. I was sorely tempted to do so. At twenty-three, the head of the psychology department at Baylor University offered me a student teaching position and a full scholarship to go directly from a B.S. to a Ph.D. We all knew I could succeed. I turned him down and stayed in the Air Force.

Instead, I pursued an M.S. (Master of Science) in systems management at the Air Force Institute of Technology, with an undeclared minor in Operations Research, an M.P.M. (Master of Pastoral Ministry) at Seattle University, and a diploma in Spiritual Direction from the Monastery of the Risen Christ. Why pass up the Ph.D.? Because I knew myself.

I am a generalist, not a specialist. Rather than work at great depth in one or two fields, my gift is a capacity to integrate across a multitude of specialty fields, to coordinate between disciplines and achieve organization goals beyond individual capacities. I am at my best as a manager, commander, spiritual director, and author. Example? My third book is described as "an interdisciplinary study of science, philosophy, and contemporary mores." Wide ranging, eh?

To devote my life to one field would have led to professional death from acute boredom. In the Air Force, many varieties of accomplishment were laid out before me in radar engineering, system program management, space operations, base command, and strategic planning. I moved through all these endeavors almost at whim, with official meritorious results!

You, too, need to assess your general limits, capacities and nature. That is an important contribution and foundation to authentic humility.

To conclude, find the narrow gate by clearing away any sins that haunt you. Perhaps you already have. If not, work on it. Then, prepare to open the narrow gate by first applying the oil of your own <u>authentic</u> humility. We will free that upper hinge in Week IV. Ronda?

Ronda's Encouragement

Over many years, I have discovered subtle forms of the deadly sin of pride that permeate my way of thinking. Before being able to beg for grace to change, I had to become aware of such patterns.

Here are two of them you might be able to identify with yourself:

- Exceptionality. This word is used by the psychiatrist, Dr. Abraham Low, founder of Recovery, International for anger, fear, and depression. Low claimed that one source of fear and anger and depression was what he called "exceptionality". Most of the time we perform in an average manner, and our lives go along in their exterior details in an average way. But those who think themselves "exceptional" feel grieved and angry whenever we don't do things perfectly or when others don't do things perfectly. And we feel fearful, when we face challenges where we might appear to be merely average instead of exceptional!

  Now, another word for "exceptionality" is pride! Getting angry because things don't go my way so that I can seem exceptional reveals an underlying pride in self. On average, some things go my way and many don't. A humble person accepts that average and doesn't get angry and depressed every time something doesn't turn out wonderfully.

Becoming aware of this pattern in my frequent bouts of anger helps me recognize that I get angry because things are not going my way, and asking God for the grace to offer up frustrations, avoiding angry reactions.

By the way, when a priest spiritual director told me, "Ronda, I can absolve you of sins of anger, but you need to get to the bottom of it." I felt obliged to at least try Recovery International (not a 12-step program); a system of dealing with anger, fear, and depression. After 10 years of these groups, I went from five fits of anger a day to two a week. My family loved this system that helped me victimize them less!

- Drama Queen Scenarios. Another way I understand the deadly sin of pride and the anger that comes from pride, I call the "drama queen scenario." According to this way of thinking, I am the heroine of the drama of life. Y'all are either secondary characters or walk-on's. Your role is to enhance my life. If you fail to make this your priority, then I throw a fit!!!

The humble person thinks of God as the center of life and we are secondary characters trying to do God's will together moment by moment. By contrast, I can act as if when I have a tech problem, since I am the queen, all my techie relatives and friends have to drop what they are doing and immediately help me. By contrast, I need to commend the problem to God, the center of my life, and ask for help in a soft voice, waiting calmly for help.

For Personal Reflection and Group Sharing

- Did any of the insights in this third week stand out for you?

- Of the deadly sins: pride, envy, anger, laziness, avarice, gluttony, envy, to which one of these are you most given or by which most tempted? What spiritual practices have helped you in the past to open to more grace for overcoming such tendencies?
- Can you think of examples in your own life where you have failed to see your limitations and later regretted it?
- Can you compose a prayer to say when your worst traits tempt you?

"Loving humility is a terrible force: whenever we give up anything or suffer anything, not with a sense of rebellious bitterness, but willing out of love, this makes us not weaker but stronger...the power of God is shown...in the fact that out of love God has emptied himself (Philippians 2:7) has poured himself out in generous self-giving, by His own free choice...God is never so strong as when he is most weak."
 - Bishop Callistos Ware, *The Orthodox Way*

WEEK IV

Obey the Commandments of God

Truly... the recompense is great for those who keep your commandments. If you are wise, then, know that you have been created for the Glory of God and your own eternal salvation. This is your goal; this is the center of your life; this is the treasure of your heart. If you reach this goal, you will find happiness. If you fail to reach it, you will find misery.
- Robert Bellarmine, Bishop and Doctor

Decision #4:
To Obey God's Will.

In California, my wife and I often

attended the annual Southern California Renewal Conference at Anaheim. One particular year, our friend Fr. Bob Lussier was giving his first, ever, conference talk to about 300 of the attendees in a grand ballroom. Wall to wall folks. We got there right at the introduction, sitting in the last vacant chairs in the back-right corner near the door. About ten minutes into his talk, Fr. Bob casually mentioned the word "obedience." Fifteen people (I count *everything* out of a habit from my early teens of counting railroad cars pulled by steam locomotives!) – fifteen people abruptly stood bolt upright, grabbed their belongings and stalked out of the room, passing nearby us with lockjaw grim, angry faces.

Just on that word – obedience! Fr. Bob had not yet fully expressed his intended context. It was clear to everyone: for those fifteen, obedience was a four-letter word. Fr. Bob and the entire crowd watched the exodus in silence. Then he said, "See, exactly what I was getting to. Aversion to obeying the objective truth even among Church members. He then continued his presentation against relativism, the belief in our culture that there are no moral absolutes, so each person may define his own truth. That what is right or wrong is relative to one's own cultural programming. He ended to a standing ovation!

Satan can even clothe himself in the cloak of humility, but he does not know how to wear the cloak of obedience.
- Sister Faustina's Diary

But for the authentic Christian, there is only one ultimate Truth, and he is a person. It behooves us to obey him. He, himself incarnate, also had only one ultimate Truth; the will of the Father, for whom he spoke.

Are you seeking holiness? Do you desire to "see" God? Yes? Free the upper hinge of the narrow gate with the oil of obedience! Consider the following scripture, one of the most important passages in the New Testament!

They who have my commandments and keep them are those who love me, and those who love me will be loved by my Father, and I will love them and reveal myself to them.

- John 14:21

This short passage of Scripture is an essential definition of what it means to love God. I personally testify to it. He *does* reveal Himself to the obedient in a way and time of his choosing. It's all about obedience! Many have learned to "see" God; testify to an awareness of His active presence.

You may be thinking, sure, I have to obey God, but do I have to obey every authority figure who tries to force me to do something I don't want to do? The general rule is to obey competent authorities to whom you are accountable, operating within their area of authority and expertise; ordering or recommending a legal and moral course of action. This is true in the American military, in government, in the Church, and is a wise rule to follow; convenient or not. In regard to the Church and our topic, it is good to have a spiritual director or friend who can help you sort out the issues and make the wise choice: to obey or go your own way. Of course, a spiritual director has moral, but not binding, authority over you. You would be in a voluntary relationship.

In Week II, we suggested detachment from wealth, power, and the easy life. You might want to go back and review. But we left a fourth way of detachment hanging. This is a good time to bring up the last form of detachment.

> *But detachment of will is the hardest, most necessary, and most meritorious detachment; the fully detached person leaves himself unreservedly in God's hands, "not as I will, but as thou wilt."*
> - *A Catholic Dictionary*, p 145

You are well aware that Jesus summarized all the commandments in two parts: love God with all your heart (of which obedience is the essential part); and love your neighbor as yourself.

In this regard, you truly have embraced Catholic life and culture (Week I). You attend and celebrate Mass regularly as often as possible; you are carefully listening to homilies; you are reading scripture and commentaries; you are going to confession regularly, discriminating between good and evil in your daily life, have you not? We need not provide here a long, detailed list of commandments.

You have detached authentically from wealth, power, and the easy life (Week II), have you not?

And you have found the narrow gate, applying the oil of authentic humility to that lower hinge (Week III), have you not? To open the narrow gate, now you must apply the holy oil of obedience to that upper hinge.

It is time to reflect on God's will by category. God's will is perfect or positive, and God's will is permissive. What is the difference?

God's perfect will is expressed by divine revelation as contained in the Old Testament and in the ministry of Jesus as passed to us in Christian Scripture, the *Catechism of the Catholic Church*, writings of the Saints and Doctors of the Church, and the teachings of the Catholic

Magisterium. One fully appreciates the value of these teachings by living an active, sacramental life within the Church in accordance with the Magisterium (Week I). The call to obey God's perfect will is obvious. See quote, above. (They who have my commandments, etc.)

God's perfect or positive will is also in the realities of design and function inherent to the universe as expressed through its physical laws and mathematical constants of the universe. But permissive will?

God's permissive will is whatever actually happens day-to-day that is not caused or intended by him. That is to say, what he allows, but not necessarily intends. We are very happy when God permits good things to happen to us individually, such as being assigned a task that we enjoy, or receiving recognition and a promotion.

The problem comes when we see that good things happen to bad people and bad things happen to good people; often we do not see our own plans fulfilled. "Man proposes; God disposes!" Hurricanes and wars happen. Pain and suffering and disappointments are part of life. We all die.

God allows events that we count as disasters. *"Shall we receive the good at the hand of God and not receive the bad?* Job 2:10. God allows much that we consider to be bad. Why?

It's partly about the physical laws and mathematical constants of universal design. Physical laws and twenty universal mathematical constants keep order in the universe. We need a stable, anthropic (life sustaining) universe. The laws and constants of our anthropic universe will not be adjusted for our convenience. Universal chaos resulting from a change of physical laws or constants would destroy all life. A few examples: what if gravity oscillated between positive and negative, dragging you down, then throwing you up into the air and back down again? What if time reversed at random moments? What if ice sank instead of floating? The oceans would have filled up with ice, bottom to top, eons ago. No life ever would be in, or come from the ocean! What if the universe was filled with black holes?

It's also about free will which defines us as human in the image and likeness of God.

But other folks have their own free will; have conflicting ideas, understandings, and goals. They often disagree with or work against us. Life can be messy and aggravating. All of us tend to grumble at the permissive will of God when things don't go our way!

Here is a little test. Do you seriously grumble or rail when you are cut off in traffic or miss a green light and are delayed? Not so close relatives or acquaintances arrive at your door unannounced. You had other plans. Do you grumble to yourself? Respond curtly? The baby awakes you at 3am. Are you loving or abrupt with the baby? Your husband brings home a guest without warning, just as you come from the bathroom, half dressed. Are you angry at your husband? You might have asked him to warn you ahead of time by speaking the truth with love rather than anger.

You can think of a thousand examples from your day-to-day life. The trip you planned gleefully falls through. You respond with anger? Think of a few of your pet peeves.

Now consider. When you are grumbling over some unanticipated inconvenience or suffering some disaster which you cannot avoid or change, are you not resisting reality? Are you not placing yourself in opposition to God's permissive will? Is that obedience?

This type of disobedience in opposition and response to reality is a major source of unhappiness. If you fight reality habitually, you seldom will be happy. Totally accepting obedience to God, even his permissive will, is peace and a major step toward holiness.

If you peacefully accept and respond to all the consequences of God's positive and permissive will, adjusting and responding peacefully to reality as it is moment-to-moment, you liberally have applied the oil of obedience to the upper hinge. Now you may swing wide the narrow gate onto the holy mountain of God.

So far, we have spoken of God's will in categories and everyone's necessary response. But what if God has a specific will for you? Just you alone? Week V is dead ahead. Ronda?

Ronda's Encouragement

For my husband and I, the most difficult time of having to respond to God's permissive will was when our son committed suicide at age 20. Our first babies were twin girls. Then came several miscarriages and then Charlie. He was a loveable, generally obedient child, a favorite at school among classmates. We didn't realize until after his death that he was hiding severe depression and schizophrenic tendencies.

I have written a whole book called *Weeping with Jesus; the Journey from Grief to Hope* (St. Louis, MO: En Route Books and Media, 2016) using descriptions of our sorrows and eventual healing concerning Charlie's suicide.

For the purposes of Week IV's reflections, I want to focus on this alleged message from Jesus to me after months of acute agonizing grief. "I allowed Charlie to take his life because of his great pain. His joys were a foretaste of heaven; his sorrows weaned him from this earth. You will find him in my Sacred Heart."

These consoling words gave me hope, even though such a death is an arrow in the heart that never goes away from every parent, I guess, until reunion in heaven.

Please notice the wording of this message in relationship to the question of obedience to God's perfect or permissive will. Never is a sin such as suicide the perfect will of God! However, he permitted it to happen.

Obedience to God's permissive will in this tragic, dramatic happening, meant that I could not "blame" God for letting Charlie kill himself, as some who grieve feel tempted to do.

As in: "God, you could have arranged that my father leave the house five minutes later so the murderous thief would not have killed him on the way to his car. Why didn't you do that? Didn't omniscient you, God, know how shattered our family would be by the death of our beloved father?

"Why did the tornado hit our house and not the house next door? Do you love them more than us?"

When people ask me if I was mad at God because of Charlie's suicide, I like to quip,

"As a convert from an atheistic background, I am so glad that God exists, how could I be mad at him?"

Pastoral counselors, however, consider it quite normal and sometimes necessary for some grievers to vent their anger at God and so to speak, wrestle with him, as did Jacob of the Old Testament, until God gives them some answer that satisfies them.

I often say that this earth is not our home. For the good and the repentant, this earth is but a testing ground for heaven. Meditating on how we will see those for whom we pray, someday in eternity, goes a long way to assuage grief.

Another example, much more trivial, but more constant for me, is to accept God's permissive will in the matter of frustrating annoyances of tech. As is true of many older people, the computer came upon us when we were already middle-aged. Some typists just quit their jobs rather than deal with the new technology!

To cope with my almost daily rage at the computer and the smart phone, I often ask myself questions such as these:

Would I really be happier to live in a

swamp in a jungle where there was no tech but only snakes and giant insects?

Would I really want to give up all the advantages of tech such as sending chapters in manuscripts to a publisher in one click instead of typing them out and then putting them through an ugly purple printing mimeograph machine?

Can I not accept that you, God of Providence, wished me to live from 1937 to whenever I die in a high tech culture with all its advantages as well as disadvantages?

To tell you the truth, even though I have analyzed such big and little crosses to death, it never occurred to me until reading Al Hughes' Week IV that resistance to what God has allowed in his permissive will is a form of disobedience!

The reason is partly that, as is probably true of many of our readers, I tend to be very obedient to the moral and liturgical directions of the Church. But that is the challenge of Week I, and now by Week IV, if I want to grow in holiness on the journey up the Mountain of God, I need fresh challenges about accepting God's permissive will.

For Personal Reflection and Group Sharing

- Looking at your life, what are some of the experiences of obedience and disobedience to authorities such a parents, teachers, bosses, police, or priests, that stand out for you in your life?
- What insights about obedience in Al Hughes' explanation seem important for you to consider?
- What are instances of rejecting or accepting the permissive will of God that you have struggled with in the past or present?
- Can you compose a prayer about obedience?

"What else is knowledge of the Father but the recognition of him through whom this knowledge comes to us? He, himself, declares 'everyone who acknowledges me, I in my turn will acknowledge in the presence of the Father. This, then, will be our reward if we acknowledge him

through whom we have been saved. But how shall we know that we acknowledge him? By doing what he says, not by disobeying his commands, and by honoring him not only with our lips but with our whole heart and our whole mind...for he says in Isaiah: 'This people pays me lip service, but its heart is far from me.'"

- From a homily written in the 2nd Century, *Liturgy of the Hours*, Monday of the 32nd Week in Ordinary Time

WEEK V

Follow the Leading of God

*Today, listen to the voice of the Lord:
Do not grow stubborn, as your fathers
did in the wilderness, when at Meriba
and Massah they challenged me and
provoked me, although they had seen
all of my works.*

- Psalm 95

Decision #5:
To Determine God's will for me.

Jeannie, my deceased wife, used to say, "God has a plan for everyone; God has a plan." She said that off and on throughout our 48 years of married life. She could say that based on an assessment of her own life experiences. She had a lot of good company in that belief. From religious scholars to congregation back benchers, many Christians believe so and will say it. "God has a plan for everyone!"

Your challenge is to discover and live in obedience according to God's plan for you. That it can be discovered in tried and true ways will be explained. But first, an assumption: that you have taken seriously the call to God's perfect will and permissive will which applies to everyone (Week IV). If you are working toward obedience in that regard, then also consider his specific will for you and you alone.

Listen to the voice of the Lord: but know that the Lord speaks in various ways. Not everyone, in fact a relative few, may hear his voice in the sense of hearing an audible voice, but he does convey his personalized will for you in a variety of ways. Getting a message in the heart without a sound is more common than you might think.

For the sake of discussion, God's plan for you involves one, two, or three levels of obedience open to you: a basic level for all, a second level which introduces the art of watchfulness, and a third level which requires unconditional obedience with an understanding of the consequences of operating at that level. For completeness, the discussion will end with a brief comment on Christian mysticism, what it is and what it is not; and an introduction to discernment. There are many books written on these two subjects.

The basic level relates to our discussion regarding humility (Week III): The need to assess your strengths and weaknesses in regard to gifts, talents, skills, education, insights, and background. These are basic to who you are, now. Authentic humility as presented in Week III requires that you live and operate within the limits of your gifts, talents, skills, education, insights, and background. That does not prevent you from further personal development, as mentioned in Week III. We are all called by God to rise above our initial circumstances as best we can. As you mature in age and experience, your personal assessment and boundaries of authentic humility well may expand.

The general idea of this basic level starts with a comment made by Bishop Z_____ at a retreat I attended long ago. He said, "If you love your work, it's your work. If you hate your work, it's someone else's work." That is to say, if you love your work, you likely are exercising your best gifts, talents, etc. If you do not like your work, you probably are out of line with your best gifts, talents, etc. The work you love is a good partial indication of God's will for you. One could say you are listening to the Lord who speaks through the joy and peace you find in a particular type of work.

Now-a-days, there is little excuse for not understanding who we are and are not. Any community college or university likely will administer to you any number of psychological intelligence, aptitude, and preference tests that will identify with precision who you are and what type of work or career you most would enjoy.

As an example, I took a most interesting test mid-way through my USAF career, as I began to consider my post active duty options. The test showed that I had a wide range of possibilities and would thoroughly enjoy work in systems operations, intellecttual pursuits, and the arts. But the test confirmed that I would be miserable as an accountant, in any clerical work (any routine repetitive work) or as a trade craft laborer. Dead on! In the USAF, I was already involved in space systems operations and the intellectual pursuits of strategic planning, my M.S. and mathematical studies, etc. I was excelling at these pursuits and loving it! Arts were also my passion, which most recently is expressed in my love of landscape paintings, classical music, jazz, and my own writing efforts. (I also am tinkering with the classical guitar.)

God rejoices in a joyful, obedient, and charitable disciple.

+

<u>Watchfulness</u> is an art. It can be developed sufficiently to track, day-to-day at some level of skill, God's evolving will for you. But first, since we are talking about God's plan, we need to recall there are two types of plans: straight-line planning and what is called "Lewis and Clark planning".

(Lewis and Clark led the first expedition to seek a land route across North America from St Louis to the Pacific. They followed rivers into unexplored territory. Starting with the Missouri river, if a particular river proved not to flow generally from the West, they backed up and tried another river. In this way, eventually they established a pioneer route to Oregon and the Pacific.)

A straight-line plan is simple: We first accomplish A, then B, then C, etc., continuing to some final objective. There are no alternatives to the plan, and it proceeds step-by-step to some goal or to failure.

"Lewis and Clark planning" is more like exploration. We plan to go this way, but if that does not work, we back up and try another route or strategy. God, it would seem, has to be a Lewis and Clark planner. Why?

Because often we confuse or ignore or do not understand what he would have us do. We don't see the signals, we don't listen well or consistently to God. In trying to obey God, we make mistakes.

"The monks in Egypt are said to offer frequent prayers, but these are very short and hurled like swift javelins. Otherwise, their watchful attention, a very necessary quality for anyone at prayer, could be

dulled and could disappear through protracted delays."
- St. Augustine, letter to Proba in Liturgy of the Hours, Monday, 29th Week in Ordinary Time.

Watchfulness is an art that must be learned, and we are bound to make mistakes. But you *can* learn. It is similar to the military's "situational awareness." Know what is going on around you! Here are two explanations, similar, but expressed from radically different backgrounds. A general explanation is offered by William James, a noted philosopher and psychologist at the beginning of the 20th century.

As a rule, religious persons generally assume that whatever natural facts connect themselves in any way with their destiny are significant of the divine purpose with them. Through prayer the purpose, often far from obvious, comes home to them, and if it be "trial', strength to endure the trial is given. The fundamental religious point is that in prayer, spiritual energy, which otherwise would slumber, does become active, and spiritual work of some kind is effected really.

- William James, *Varieties of Religious Experience* (New York: Longmans, Green: 1904)

Example: In process of my miraculous conversion from agnosticism at the end of November, 1978, I was praying repeatedly over several days that a monsoonal rain at Antigua, West Indies, would cease in time for my elder daughter's sixth birthday party. My prayer was very specific in the date and in the beginning/ending time that I needed a dry yard for the outdoor party.

The monsoonal rain all over the northeast Caribbean was continual without break from a week before till several days after the party. It rained continually all over the northeast Caribbean during that period without letup – except that at the precise date and times for which I had prayed, it did not rain on my yard and my yard only. Not a drop. Yet, it was raining steadily all around our yard, up close and personal throughout the party. That entire event is related with great detail in my *Paradise*

Commander (Corpus Christi, Texas: Goodbooks Media, 2012.)

Pope Benedict XVI has mentioned the following in regard to the Lord's way of communicating without vocal speech.

All of us are interested in what Heaven may think...so most of us are interested in "signs". We get them in many ways...through what we read...through what others say...(through) what we see. God speaks quietly, but he gives us all kinds of signs. In retrospect, especially, we can see that he has given us a little nudge through a friend, through a book, or through what we see as a failure – even through "accidents". If we remain alert, then slowly they piece together a consistent whole, and we begin to feel how God is guiding us.
- From *Spirit Daily*, June 5, 2006

Benedict reveals the ordinary way that religious persons relate in a personal way to the Transcendent; but effectively to understand this form of prayerful dialogue, we must be careful to remain watchful and use prudent discernment. Later, we will address some general rules about discernment. Yes, watchfulness is an art; but you may master it through practice.

+

<u>Unconditional obedience</u>. So far, we have discussed the normative ways that God reveals his particular will for us, personally: a basic level of assessing our proper role in life and the further need for watchfulness so that we might obey his signals. The question now is, to what extent are we willing to obey. It is safe to assume that if your will matches God's will for you, you likely are eager to obey. But what if he indicates something you really don't want to do. What then?

Previously, I suggested that the work you love to do is a good indication of God's will for you. However, he may ask you to change in a way that you resist. If you obey anyway, you can be sure he will lead you through that undesired task to a life far more productive and enjoyable than you could have imagined. But you will have to trust and go with God.

Instead, would you begin to rationalize? "Oh, he can't really mean that!" Or "I can go just so far, but then I really can't do more!" or "He can't mean that, he must mean this!" or just ignore the whole thing and press on with your own 'druthers?

Example: At the time of my initial conversion, my wife and I, a month or two apart, had the Pentecostal experience.

When the day of Pentecost had come...suddenly from heaven there came a sound like the rush of a violent wind and it filled the house... Divided tongues, as of fire...appeared among them... All of them were filled with the Holy Spirit and began to speak in other languages, as the Spirit gave them ability. Acts 2:1-4.

My experience of this (also detailed in *Paradise Commander, chapter 8,* mentioned above) came second after my wife's experience. We then looked at each other and decided on what seemed obvious to us. We took a joint vow of *unconditional* obedience.

The challenge came three years later.

I loved my USAF career and eagerly

would have stayed on under then current rules for a total of 28 years. But just after 20 years, the Lord challenged me to retire: that early! I was devastated! I struggled and rationalized for a couple of months; but a vow is a vow, so I retired against my own will. My vow of unconditional obedience was authenticated, but I had no clue what was to come next. How would I support my family? It was a time of mixed joy, confusion and depression for me. My wife said, "Trust and go!"

As it turned out, because I obeyed, the Lord took care of everything. What followed was my M.P.M. and a good job for which I had not applied. He continued to build in me a life far above my dreams; guided me to become a catechist, retreat master, spiritual director and author: a life filled with increasing divine light! Because I obeyed.

But I warn you! The lord takes this vow most seriously. Think carefully before you take a vow of *unconditional* obedience. I also encourage you to do so; at some point, do so. It is the natural follow-on to detaching from your own will. BUT BE

SURE YOU ACTUALLY AND COMPLETELY ARE READY TO DETACH ENTIRELY FROM YOUR OWN WILL!

This is what Jesus was indicating when he required his disciples to pick up their cross, follow him, and never look back.

We vowed unaware of the consequences. Only much later did we discover that St. Jane Frances de Chantal had it all figured out.

...there is another martyrdom; the martyrdom of love. Here God keeps his servants and handmaids in this present life so that they may labor for him, and he makes them both martyrs and confessors. Yield yourself fully to God and you will find out! Divine love takes its sword to the hidden recesses of our inmost soul and divides us from ourselves: from the moment when we commit ourselves unreservedly to God, until our last breath.

I am speaking, of course, of great-souled individuals who keep nothing back for themselves, but instead are faithful in love. Our Lord does not intend this martyrdom for those who are weak in love and perseverance. Such people he lets continue on their mediocre way, so that they will not be lost to him; he never does violence to our free will. (New York: Catholic Book Publishing Company, *Liturgy of the Hours, Vol I,* Proper of Saints, December 12.)

If you truly have progressed to this point, that will be your choice: regarding obedience, to be mediocre, or be all in for love of God and neighbor. Be forewarned. The path on the mountain of God gets steep at this point. The next week takes you straight up into *unconditional* charity! May you persevere.

<u>Christian mysticism</u>. Before completing this week's walk, we must take a brief look at the reality of Christian mysticism. We have alluded to it without naming it. The casual person hearing the word "mystic" is likely to think of a half-naked, skinny old man sitting cross-legged on a hill top humming the name of some pagan god. Not so the Christian mystic. Not so. The Christian mystic professes...

...knowledge of God's presence, in which the soul has, as a great reality, a sense of contact with him. It does not necessarily

involve psycho-physical phenomena, such as visions or ecstasies... It must be accepted as genuine, because it is unanimously attested by all mystics of east and west and show(s) itself wonderfully operative of good in their lives. A "practical" character and an "objective" cast of mind are characteristic marks of the Christian mystic.

- A Catholic Dictionary, p. 337

It is also necessary to recognize that as one approaches mysticism authentically, the initiative comes from God, not from our own efforts. Through humility and obedience, we only set the stage for his call.

Finally, a few rules on discernment. For a proposed action or actual occurrence, ask the following: 1) does it make sense? 2) is it consistent with Scripture? 3) is it in accordance with the Catechism and the Magisterium? 4) is it a loving response or merely self-serving? And St. Peter's test, 5) by their fruits ye shall know them.

Ronda?

Ronda's Encouragement

In being obedient to God's will in personal decisions, I have gotten most help in discerning his will through spiritual directors. Here is a discernment that stands out in terms of explaining the process to you. As soon as my husband died, twenty years ago, I began to dream of communities I could belong to as an aspiring Sister or as a member of some group of lay Catholics. I was always attracted to lay communities, even when my husband was alive, but since he disliked all groups, I never could explore my wish.

Consulting my spiritual director, a well-known holy, mystical priest, founder of a community of priests and of sisters, he gave me this surprising advice: "Ronda, in spite of your zeal, you don't have the personality to be in a community. Forget it!"

Even though I am always obedient when it comes to God's perfect will for Catholics on general matters of faith and morals, when it comes to individual choices, I resist. In this case, as a new widow, the longing to be close to others, especially others who also wanted to become holy, was persistent. As a result, since that holy priest died shortly after his pronouncement to me, and I had other spiritual directors less sure about this matter, I tried community after community.

Each time my involvement failed, I would attribute this not to my personality, but to the failings of some of those in the community that I had wanted to join! Eventually, I would have to see that my personality traits that made community living so difficult were obvious to all but myself.

How so? Well, in a Vatican Document about community life, it is taught that to be in a community, one has to put loving relationships to the members ahead of the specific apostolate of the group. But I tend always to put the ministry goals of every group first. If it is a teaching group, then I pour all my energy into teaching; if an evangelizing group, then into that ministry.

The goals are good, and my efforts usually are good, but what is lacking is the effort of love for each of the members expressed in daily, patient, loving service and endurance of their negative traits! As well, I am quarrelsome and overly critical in anything to do with inconsistencies of members in obeying the rule of the particular community. Especially, when it comes to living simply vs. having more than needed possessions.

By contrast, spiritual directors have always urged me on in my teaching, writing, and speaking, for which God has given me many talents.

For Personal Reflection and Group Sharing

- What elements of the writings in this Week V by Al Hughes and Ronda Chervin stood out for you?
- Think of major decisions you have made in the past? Which ones seem to you to have been in obedience to God's will? Any decisions that proved not to be God's will?
- At this time in your life, should you be able to find a spiritual director or a spiritual friend, do you need to seek

the guidance of another to help you discern God's will?
- Can you write a prayer for unconditional obedience to God's will?

"Following...to the heights of God's commandments, we easily complete the race of life. For elsewhere the Apostle says: 'Let us run with fidelity the race that has been set before us, with our eyes on Jesus, the origin and goal of our faith. So, a man who openly despises the accolades of this world and rejects all earthly glory must also practice self-denial. Such self-denial means that you never seek your own will, but God's."

- St. Gregory of Nyssa: Liturgy of the Hours, Saturday, 26th Week in Ordinary Time

WEEK VI

Love of God and Neighbor Unconditionally

Love is patient; love is kind; love is not envious or boastful or arrogant or rude. It does not insist on its own way; it is not irritable or resentful; it does not rejoice in wrongdoing, but rejoices in the truth. It bears all things, believes all things, hopes all things, endures all things. Love never ends.

- 1 Cor.13: 4-8

Decision #6: To embrace *unconditional* charity.

Already, we have discussed love of God at some length; that love being expressed and affirmed by obedience to the will of God. But also, we love and obey God by loving his people. Not to do so is a serious, possibly fatal business. Nor can one hope for or profess to seek holiness while excluding any others from love.

As also it is written, *He who would be the greatest in the Kingdom of God shall be the servant of all.* That is the essence of charity, of love: servanthood expressed through loving kindness – toward **all!** As St. Paul urges, to be conscious of, to *anticipate* and serve the needs of others. Such charity has to be developed strongly enough to overcome unbridled self-gratification, pride of self; and prejudice inflicted on peoples not like yourself in race, creed, or culture – all people means all people! Servant of all! Unconditionally! *Love never ends! Love never fails!*

Or, for the unloving, *the gate is wide and the road is easy that leads to destruction, and there are many who take it.*

Unconditional charity, *loving kindness* need be expressed toward all; but that includes you! You must take care of yourself as well. Jesus commanded love of neighbor *as* yourself, not *instead* of yourself! Loving kindness neither violates prudence nor virtue nor allows disobedience to God's will. There are moral limits to be observed.

You may neither promote, nor serve nor assist anyone in an evil intent or act. Ronda provided me with an excellent example. St. Elizabeth of Portugal took care of the illegitimate children sired by her husband in his love affairs! Loving service to innocent children and perhaps loving forgiveness of the husband's sins despite his unfaithfulness. Emotionally painful, no doubt, but unconditional. But she certainly did not aid and abet his sins.

Another example, the battering husband or wife. Prudence requires separation at some level of abuse. St. Paul exhorts us to anticipate the needs of others, but he also speaks of the need to separate from non-believers and unrepentant sinners at some point.

Following are a couple of cases regarding a subtle lack of unconditional love, often overlooked or served in the breach.

How can one claim to be charitable to all, much less unconditionally so, while ignoring all but their own associates and family members <u>who happen to be like themselves?!</u>

Sometimes, truth is better served by pointing out the opposite. By comparison and contrast, the truth comes clear.

+

Case in point #1...

Long retired, I circulate primarily in Corpus Christi Church and bridge circles. I live and write downtown; I play bridge at a Methodist church and at Pius X. From time to time, someone will ask me where I go to church. The conversation usually goes something like this.

"Where do you go to church, Al?"

"I go to OLG, Our Lady of Guadalupe parish."

"Where's that?"

"Over in the west side. It's the barrio parish."

"Where?! With the *Mexicans*?!"

"Sure. Been going over there for half-a-dozen years."

"Why in the world would you want to go over there with *them!?*"

"Because I love it over there! Lots of gracious, warm folks."

That elicits a grimace or a head shake, and they drop the subject. It is the characteristic problem of the Pharisee, whom Jesus was constantly chastising. "We are the good and acceptable; *them* (Romans, Greeks, Arabs and everybody else, even other Jews who did not follow all their religious legalisms) are deficient, unacceptable." Pharisees set themselves apart as superior. They did not comprehend charity.

Sorry to inform you, but *them* on the west side is us. We all are one under God.

Borne of history and cultural differences, Corpus Christi is two cities; roughly 50/50 between Mexican-Americans and us gringos. Historically, the early settlers here were mostly Czechs. (The Germans settled up in Fredericksburg.) The Czechs found cheap land, Indians, and Mexicans already here. You occasionally hear old atrocity stories about Mexican banditos and native Americans, but you will never hear about the atrocities of early ranchers and other settlers. And there is memory of the Alamo. Just like the old south and the civil war. "Fergit? Hell!"

Voiced prejudice is almost all one way. The Indians are mostly gone; the Mexican-Americans hold the short stick. Even those Mexican-Americans who amass a modicum of wealth bail out and move to the prosperous south side. West Side is a barrio because nearly all those remaining are poor: often desperately poor mothers and grandmothers raising families without a father in the house! Cutoff by the Crosstown Freeway.

You recognize poverty immediately when you pass under the freeway and enter west side. It is like going through a curtain, into the town's back room. Neither the city administration nor most of the affluent Mexican-Americans seem to take an interest in the west side plight. The affluent leave for the south side; few look back.

Around Our Lady of Guadalupe parish, the problem of poverty is evident. (To be precise, approximately 80% are poor, most of the rest middle class). But the people of the church warmly welcomed my wife, Jeannie, and I. They talk to each other and to us, linger after mass, often are filled with solicitous concern, love, and yes, even joy! Not everyone, of course, but many.

Blessed are the poor. As a result, my wife and I jumped right in six years ago to contribute and share parish concerns, love and yes, even joy! Now, I assist as I can and Ronda, my co-author, has her own lay ministry in the same church. Blessed are the poor, whom Jesus favored.

Even though the poor are often rough and unrefined, we must not judge them from external appearances.... On the contrary, if you consider the poor in the light of faith, then you will observe that they are taking the place of the Son of God who chose to be poor. We also ought to have this same spirit and imitate Christ's actions, that is, we must take care of the poor, console them, help them, support their cause.

Charity is certainly greater than any rule. Moreover, all rules must lead to charity. Since she is a noble mistress, we must do whatever she commands.
- St. Vincent de Paul, priest

The open gate of your own charity, then, naturally follows the oils of humility and obedience which you applied to the gate hinges in earlier weeks, did you not?

When we first moved to Corpus Christi, we attended a certain parish – for three weeks we did. Coldest church we had ever had the pleasure to enter. And I don't mean the air conditioning. The place was run like a filling station. All gringos: park, rush in, listen to the basics, fill-up with Eucharist, rush out, and drive away.

We then found another Catholic church where people actually seemed to like each other, liked being there and actually lingered a bit to talk! And had active lay ministries! I competed my 25 years as a Catholic catechist there. Later, we joined the families over at Our Lady of Guadalupe.

Let us go rejoicing, to the house of the Lord.

Case in point #2...

How often do you see people walk by, ignoring you while talking on their cell telephone or nose down over a hand-held electronic device? How often have you received a look of exasperation for interrupting them with a cheerful greeting? How often do strangers smile or speak to you in the grocery or big box store? How often have you, yourself, been guilty of ignoring a friendly passerby, or not greeting them? Real and meaningful personal acknowledgement, loving conversation, new friends, and personal relations are the victims of the resulting focus in self-absorption.

And now, with the internet, we don't even venture out of our box to shop. Anything can be ordered from home sitting alone in your skivvies. Delivered in a few days. Just today, joining a line at the credit union, I said hello to a young woman in line. After a quick glance, she returned to hunt and peck on her hand-held device. She totally ignored me and everyone else in the line.

Remember watchfulness? How do you accomplish that in self-imposed isolation?

The great challenge, then, is to persevere in charity (love), when in today's culture there are so many sin-inviting distractions: not only the internet; TV programs and advertisements constantly promote self-indulgence, greed of power and of wealth, and of the easy life; vicarious sports addictions fill our free time; there are constant pressures at work to increase production while suppressing social and reflective time; a multitude of commercial entertainments designed to focus your attention on anything but the person with you. All of these distractions serve to isolate peoples, one from another. And yes, some time is appropriate spent in physical recreation and entertainment, but also the same for contemplation, prayer, and socializing.

It is true that American people are the most generous on the planet. We send billions to the needy through government and personal gifts and grants. But we ignore the poor, the addicted, and the homeless right down the street; worse, we criticize them because they somehow are different. Unconditional love?

He who would be the greatest in the Kingdom of God shall be the servant of all. That is the essence of charity, of love: servanthood expressed through loving kindness – toward *all*! How can one practice unconditional loving service through an impersonal electronic device? (Excluding the case of keeping contact with distant relatives or friends if that is the only approach available).

The Lord has been very specific about this. He has provided us a "litmus test" which must be passed for salvation, for holiness. It is as much about attitude as action applied to our daily lives.

Come you who are blessed by my Father, inherit the kingdom prepared for you from the foundation of the world; for I was hungry and you gave me food, I was thirsty and you gave me something to drink, I was a stranger and you welcomed me, I was naked and you gave me clothing, I was sick and you took care of me, I was in prison and you visited me, Mt 25:34-36.

Unconditional charity can often be a

practical matter, not all that difficult to practice. It relates to the conflict between Protestants and Catholics regarding salvation. The Protestant view is that faith alone saves. St. James, however, writes that faith without works, belief without a loving response, is dead on arrival. Here are two positive examples from my own experience.

During the late seventies, I was in command of Antigua Air Station, West Indies. The island was in transition from a British colony, working toward independence. A military uniform, British or American, announced authority: one was to be approached with respect for the power he represented and exercised. I was downtown at the capital, St. John's, in uniform and hurrying to a meeting regarding a twenty-year assignment of authorized radio frequencies; the meeting was held at the Antigua Public Utilities Authority.

Walking past a corner of the street half a block away, I was hailed by a young black Antiguan man who was crossing the street in my direction. Though rushed, I stopped and asked if I could help him. He wanted to know if he could obtain American citizenship by enlisting in the US military. I agreed that that had been possible in the 1940's, perhaps early 50's, but that was certainly no longer the case. But I said, "Tell you what. To be sure, I will call back to the States, check around and see if there still is some possible way for you to join up. Be at this corner a week from today, same time. I will be here and I will have your answer." He looked very doubtful but agreed.

I did as I said. I called military recruiters and appropriate policy offices in Florida and all the way to Washington. I spent most of an hour on multiple calls to be absolutely sure. A week later I was on that corner. I drove down town from the base several miles away specifically to meet him. And here he came, crossing the street, amazed that I was actually there.

I gave him the bad news, but I counseled him to get the best education he could obtain and work his way up in his own environment. He thanked me, we shook hands, and he crossed back over the street. I often think of him. That was 1978.

Very recently, walking to lunch

downtown, I passed a derelict building with thick waist high plants near the door. Previously, I had noticed evidence that a homeless person had slept behind those bushes. This time, out of the corner of my eye, I noticed a slight movement. Someone was sleeping there.

Continuing on, I had lunch; ordered another lunch as a takeout. Returning, I approached the bushes with an inquiring "Hello?" A pleasant looking forty something woman(!) stood up with fear etched across her face. "Sorry to bother you, but I am returning from lunch at Citrus Bistro. I thought you might be hungry." Her face went from fear to joy in a fraction of a second. When I departed, she was singing softly to herself with a broad smile, laying out a large white cloth on her blanket, like an elegant tablecloth spread in a residence she may once had enjoyed. For a little while she knew joy.

It took so little. Watchfulness, caring and ten bucks! Ronda?

Ronda's Encouragement

Without serving love, and lots of it, no one would ever be declared a saint. Even hermits alone in the desert manifest serving love in their prayers for those out in the world.

Whereas Al describes serving love shown in sacrificial deeds for others, I want to emphasize the charitable love shown in overcoming character defects that lead not only to negligence in serving others, but also to victimizing others, often in significant ways – surely a violation of the charity God wishes to us to exhibit at all times.

My recent book, *The Way of Love,* published by En Route Books and Media in 2016, is divided into these small volumes: "What is Love," "Obstacles to Love," "Making Loving Moral Decisions," and "A Hundred Day Spiritual Marathon."

Much of this book is about recognizing our short-comings so that we may be motivated to pray for the grace that God's perfect love would overcome these flaws. Of course, if God's perfect love really were flowing through us 24/7, the number of people we would hurt in one way or the other would go down to zero!

But for we, wannabe saints, who have not yet gotten to the very top of the mountain, it will always be a struggle. I have already told you about many of my own such battles with my bad characteristics. Here I want to summarize for you some of the ideas in my book *Way of Love* that readers and students have found most helpful.

- Make a scorecard for a whole day itemizing in one column loving thoughts, words, and deeds and in another column all unloving ones. Then reflect on your score.

- Ask people closest to you in the family, workplace, or parish to tell you what they think to be three very loving traits of yours. Then ask them to tell you about one unloving trait. On the unloving traits that surface, with the help of a spiritual director, mentor or friend, look for the psychological root of that trait. (For example, since my mother was very critical of everyone, I tend to be also.) Then, bring the unloving trait to prayer and beg God for the grace to replace it with its charitable opposite. (I beg God to make me less critical and more patient and understanding about the defects of others.) Then try for a week to struggle with that negative trait by praying for the grace of charity in the circumstances with often lead you to be unloving.

- Forgive everyone who has hurt you in your whole life, praying to God to help you do this. What helps many of my readers to forgive is to think about the long-term struggles the person who hurt them had in their own lives, such as being verbally abusive because one of their parents was verbally abusive and hurt them the same way they hurt you.

For Personal Reflection and Group Sharing

- Where have you gone out of your way to be of charitable service to others?
- Have you ever had to overcome a prejudice against a group of people?
- Try one of Ronda's suggestions and share your experience with others in a group or with one friend if you are not reading *Simple Holiness* in a group setting.
- Write a prayer that God would help you overcome obstacles to charity.

"When the Spirit of God descends upon a man and overshadows him with the fullness of his outpouring, then his soul overflows with joy not to be described, for the Holy Spirit turns to joy whatever he touches.

The Kingdom of Heaven is peace and joy in the Holy Spirit.

Acquire inward peace, and thousands around you will find their salvation."

- St. Seraphim of Sarov

VII. Remain on the Heights

The kingdom of God is not a matter of eating or drinking, but of justice, peace, and the joy that is given by the Holy Spirit.
- Rom. 14:17

"Joy is not a virtue distinct from charity, but an act or effect of charity."
- St. Thomas Aquinas, *A Catholic Dictionary*, p. 269

Joy in this Christian sense is not simply being extra happy or even giddily happy. It is a sustained level of calm, peaceful joy in good times and in bad, even in the face of persecution, torture, and martyrdom. St. Lawrence, as an extreme example, joked with his torturers while they were baking him alive. He told them he was done on that side. Time to turn him over!

Such joy against the reality of what actually is happening at the time is against all normal human understanding; it can be explained as a grace received from the Holy Spirit, an effect of unconditional charity. St. Lawrence actually loved and forgave his torturers. As did Christ.

A further note regarding the significance of the washing of feet. In Jesus' time, it was the slaves who had that task. They alone would wash the feet of their master. So symbolically, Christ was placing himself as the slave of his Apostles, of his Church, in humility and obedience – the two hinges of the narrow gate! *...who would be the greatest in the Kingdom of God shall be the servant of all.*

+

If you have reached this chapter and have to some extent accepted and incurporated the six recommended decisions of simple holiness, you may visualize yourself on a high ridge overlooking the "valley of the shadow of death." Do you wish to return down slope? If not, continue upward to ever higher ridges. Each higher ridge is marked by greater assurance, greater joy. The peak is up there above the clouds, in heaven: the beatific vision.

This is true in spite of set-backs, where because of terrible crosses and tragedies, you may feel yourself far from holiness as you struggle every day with temptations to despair. You will find, however, that when God's grace brings you through each part of your journey, that there were moments along the way of joy and hope, even in the midst of great sadness, doubt, and uncertainty.

As you struggle to reach a higher ridge, on the strength that results from your earlier battles against negative emotions, there will come a time when the valley recedes. At this point you will recognize the grace which is constant joy.

After all, you have entered upon a life time journey. Each higher ridge offers a more breathtaking view as confidence, perseverance, and joy increase.

Just think of the constant joy that our mother, Mary, felt after the Resurrection!

+

Perfect love casts out all fear. My wife died late in July, 2015. Alzheimer's. Earlier, on diagnosis, her neurologist forecast her remaining life at ten to fifteen years. She was gone in four. Shortly after the diagnosis, still able, she wrote her life testimony for the edification of our children and her siblings. She remained externally calm, joyful, and loving, without fear; exercising servanthood within the limits of her declining capacity all the way to the end. If she experienced fear or dread, she never spoke of it but accepted the reality of her decline. Not that she did not suffer.

She went through all the stages familiar to relatives of Alzheimer's suffers. She just never complained about it. The loss for words to express herself. The decline of memory. One evening, I offered to go to the store to get her favorite sherbet. She had no idea what I was talking about. If she wanted to go somewhere, we played 20 questions until I named the right place and she said yes. She tried to eat and maintain her strength, but her body began to reject specific foods, then everything. She had several bad falls.

Finally, she was bedridden. Starvation, the characteristic mode of death, set in. Oddly enough, during those last 40 days and 40 nights of starvation, those were her happiest, during which she was expressing joy until the total weakness of the last few days. Never through it all, a single complaint!

At her death, to her life testimony I added commentary addressed to a wider audience, also providing information about her last days. I published it as *Saint Jeannie's Shiny Black Shoes*. (Corpus Christi, Texas: Goodbooks Media, 2015).

I do not call her "saint" through any casual or careless thought. She personified selfless charity throughout the 48 years that I knew her: in Antigua, West Indies, she was equally charitable to General officers, British Governors, Premiers, government ministers, and American Ambassadors; and to our maid and half-blind elderly gardener: later, in the States, also to dying HIV patients, homeless street children, and incarcerated teens. All alike: totally consistent, totally charitable to all ... *who would be the greatest in the Kingdom of God shall be the servant of all.*

Typical of an Alzheimer's death, she died of starvation and dehydration. Not that she did not want food and water, but her body absolutely refused them. It was shutting down. The last 24 hours were a horror. I was there at the end, and I never want to see that agony in anyone, ever again. Even after the attending hospice nurse said, "She's gone," the body continued to struggle for life, though there was no breath. It took a half hour for the body's last jerking attempt to live.

And yet, during the last week, the hospice ladies became more and more concerned; not with her, but with me. Finally, the day before Jeannie died, the lead woman looked closely into my face with a most worried look and said, "Why do you seem so happy?"

There were many human reasons to be sorrowful, but she was right. I was joyful, energized, exultant! The answer I gave that afternoon was totally inadequate. I expressed only a limited understanding, myself. I mentioned the virtue of detachment which enabled me to make the necessary decisions and arrangements with a clear head despite the fact that I was losing my life partner with whom I had been inseparable for 48 years. From then on, I would have to go it alone.

I could have said, explaining our vows of obedience, "We had met every commitment we made to God in his expressed will, to our children in their care and education and to one another in chaste, faithful, and undying love. For the 37 years after our Pentecost, we had kept our vow of unconditional obedience and had worked hard, and yes, joyfully "in the vineyard," to fulfill the specific will of God for us.

You may be thinking, just as the hospice lady seemed to think, "Horrors! He is happy to be getting rid of her!" But that was not the issue at all. In the sense of human happiness, yes. I was happy that her terrible suffering was almost over. Yes, I was happy and thankful for her triumphant life in the Holy Spirit; yes, I was happy in my assurance that she would receive the crown of sanctity. Yes, in my hope to follow her into the heavenly rest.

But no, not happy at all with my loss. We had been inseparable from the first date. For 48 years we had had an adventurous life; faced death together on a number of occasions. I was her strength and she was mine. And we had just gone through four years of her rapid decline. I lost the center point of my life. Our relationship was biblical. Two had become as one and now half of me was leaving.

+

It has been two years and a little more. I still have moments of memory; going out from my little apartment. I have moments of "She was with me the last time I was here." Or, "I wish she were here, she would have enjoyed this!" Then, I remember, she certainly is enjoying heaven.

It is not my nature to cry. But I have had moments of wet eyes, melancholy, sadness, of "if only!" I look at my younger daughter, and I see Jeannie. They were more like twins than mother and daughter. And Katie even sounds like her mom. Same joyful, good humored response to life. Katie is a hard-working evangelist in her own right.

I remember Jeannie dancing with our maid in the living room. Slowly dying, yet gleeful. I remember the joy of her life and mine. I speak of her at any and all occasions. I miss her. Weepy? Holding back as I type. Hard to see the screen.

<u>Detachment</u> and fulfilled commitment (<u>obedience</u>) are part of my answer, but it goes much farther. Detachment is only collaborating evidence of true joy attained. Another factor was Jeannie's own will. When, clearly, she knew she was close to dying, repeatedly, she said to the attending doctor (in my presence), "I just want to see Jesus!" In that regard, I was happy that she was getting her heart's desire. That gave me considerable comfort. But that, too, was my happiness, not the final grace of constant spiritual joy.

The cause of true spiritual joy is a particular God-given grace. I did not know to ask for it, and I was totally surprised when I finally realized it. It was freely given; a sign of God's own love for an obedient servant, a sign of God's own <u>charity</u> at a time of our spousal separation according to His will. It is the gift of <u>sustained</u> joy in good times and bad. It is still with me. It sustains me to know that if only I persevere, as Jeannie now knows, a share in the divine nature eventually will be mine, it is just ahead on the road up the mountain of God.

... you who have fled a world corrupted by lust might become sharers of the divine nature. This is reason enough for you to make every effort to undergird your virtue with faith, your discernment with virtue, and your self-control with discernment; this self-control, in turn, should lead to perseverance, and perseverance to piety, and piety to care for your brother, and care for your brother, to love.

- 2 Pet 1:4-7

Indeed, the above underlined sequence: of unconditional detachment, humility, unconditional obedience, unconditional charity, and sustained joy – the logical sequence of *Simple Holiness* – *is* the road to a share in the nature of God, a beginning share in the divine life - a constant spiritual joy. I also said to the hospice lady, "For 48 years, I have stood with a living saint. What's not to like?"

St. Thomas says, "Joy is... an act or effect of charity. Sustained, unconditional charity leads to sustained, unconditional joy; a share in the authentic image and likeness of God.

You, too, may walk upon, remain upon the heights. We have left you a trail to follow. I know you can do it. Now I *expect* you actually to do it! One step at a time; walk on the mountain of God.

Whoever is in Christ is a new creation; the old has passed away. "Now by the 'new creation' Paul means the indwelling of the Holy Spirit in a heart that is pure and blameless, free from all malice, wickedness or shamefulness. For when a soul has come to hate sin and delivered itself as far as it can to the power of virtue, it undergoes a transformation by receiving the grace of the Spirit. Then it is healed, restored and made wholly new. Indeed, the two texts

'Purge out the old leaven that you may be a new one' and 'Let us celebrate the festival, not with the old leaven but with the unleavened bread of sincerity and truth' support those passages which speak about the new creation.

- Saint Gregory of Nyssa, bishop.

And what about my beloved wife?

When you are feeling only your losses, then everything around you speaks of them...the trees, the flowers, the clouds, the hills and valleys, they will reflect your sadness. They all become mourners...the winds whisper her name, the branches, heavy with leaves, weep for her...but as you keep walking forward with someone at your side, opening your heart, the mysterious truth that your friends death was not just the end but also a new beginning, not just the cruelty of fate, but the necessary way to freedom, not just an ugly and gruesome destruction, but a suffering leading to glory, then you gradually discern a new song sounding through creation, and going home corres-

ponds to the deepest desire of your heart.
— Henri Nouwen

Perfect love casts out all fear.
Walk the Mountain! Be transformed!
TO KNOW AND NOT TO DO, IS NOT
YET TO KNOW.

Ad Majorem Dei Gloriam.

Dedicated to the Holy Spirit, bond of love between the Father and the Son: Al Hughes and Ronda Chervin.

ADDENDA

PRAYER OF ASCENT

by Al Hughes

As we ascend your holy mountain, O Lord,
as we rise from the valley of the shadow of death,
free us from the clawing grasp of self-judgment.

Cast off from us the heavy baggage of valley needs;
suppress our inordinate desire for
wealth, or power, or an easy life of comfort.
All these things are an illusion, a vanity.

Calm our passions and desires.
They pass.
They, too, are an illusion, a vanity.

As we ascend, give us clear vision
to follow those on the path above,
but not forget aid to those who follow behind.

Give us clear wisdom
to follow your call to the mountain top,
the call of your will alone.

Help us to live that joy
beyond all understanding
in unconditional obedience and charity
in our reflection of your truth.

+

"Know that you give me greater glory by a single act of obedience than by long prayers and mortifications."
- St. Maria Faustina (Diary 894)

"One prayer from an obedient person is worth 100,000 from one who is not."
- St. Colette

"Faith makes nothing impossible and renders meaningless such words as anxiety, danger, and fear; so that the believer goes through life calmly and peacefully, with profound joy – like a child hand in hand with its mother."
- Blessed Charles de Foucauld

Letter to Autolycus from Saint Theophilus of Antioch, Bishop

"It is like this. Those who can see with the eyes of their bodies are aware of what is happening in this life on earth. The same is true of the sounds that we hear. So it is with the ears of our heart and the eyes of our mind in their capacity to hear or see God. God is seen by those who have the capacity to see him, provided that they keep the eyes of their mind open.

All have eyes, but some have eyes that are shrouded in darkness, unable to see the light of the sun. Because the blind cannot see it, it does not follow that the sun doesn't shine. The blind must trace the cause back to themselves and their eyes. In the same way, you have eyes in your mind that are shrouded in darkness because of your sins and evil deeds.

A person's soul should be clean, like a mirror reflecting light. If there is rust on the mirror his face cannot be seen in it. In the same way, no one who has sin within him can see God.

But if you will you can be healed. Hand

yourself over to the doctor. It is God who heals and gives life through his Word and his wisdom.

If you understand this, and live in purity and holiness and justice, you may see God. But, before all, faith and the fear of God must take the first place in your heart, and then you will understand all this.

When you have laid aside mortality and been clothed with immortality then you will see God according to your merits. God raises up your flesh to immortality along with your soul, and then, once made immortal, you will see the immortal One, if you believe in him now."

+

Psalm 40

I waited patiently for the Lord;
He inclined to me and heard my cry.
He drew me up from the desolate pit,
out of the miry bog,
and set my feet upon a rock,
making my steps secure.

Simple Holiness

He put a new song in my mouth,
a song of praise to our God.
Many will see and fear,
and put their trust in the Lord.

You have multiplied, O Lord, my God,
your wondrous deeds
and your thoughts towards us;
none can compare with you.

Were I to proclaim and tell of them,
they would be more than can be counted.
I delight to do your will, O my God;
your law is within my heart.

I have told the glad news of deliverance
in the great congregation;
see, I have not restrained my lips,
as you know, O Lord.

I have not hidden your saving help within
my heart,
I have spoken of your faithfulness and your
salvation;
I have not concealed your steadfast love
and your faithfulness from the great
congregation.

But may all who seek you
rejoice and be glad in you;
may those who love your salvation
continually,
"Great is the Lord!"

SOME OTHER BOOKS BY ALBERT HUGHES

Paradise Commander (Corpus Christi, Texas: Good Books Media, 2012)
St. Jeannie's Shiny Black Shoes - my deceased wife's life testimony (Corpus Christi, Texas: Good Books Media, 2015)
Buddy, Can you Spare a "Digm" – Confronting the Apocalypse of Indifference (Corpus Christi, Texas: Good Books Media, 2016)
Ice Fog, Spirit Fire, and the Narrow Gate – autobiography – (St. Louis, MO: En Route Books and Media, 2018)

SOME OTHER BOOKS BY RONDA CHERVIN

En Route to Eternity – autobiography (New York: Miriam Press, 1994)
Spirituality for all Times: Readings from the Catholic Classics co-author Kathleen Brouillette (St. Louis, MO: En Route Books and Media, 2015)
Avoiding Bitterness in Suffering: How our Heroes in Faith found Peace amid

Sorrow (Manchester, N.H.: Sophia Institute Press, 2015)

The Way of Love: The Path of Inner Transformation (St. Louis, MO: En Route Books and Media, 2017)

For other books of Ronda Chervin, visit rondachervin.com)

ALSO CO-AUTHORED BY ALBERT HUGHES AND RONDA CHERVIN

Escaping Anxiety along the Road to Spiritual Joy (St. Louis, MO: En Route Books and Media, 2017)

www.ingramcontent.com/pod-product-compliance
Lightning Source LLC
Chambersburg PA
CBHW051653040426
42446CB00009B/1110